LANDF🌐RMS

RIVERS

SANDY SEPEHRI

Rourke
Publishing LLC
Vero Beach, Florida 32964

www.rourkepublishing.com

PHOTO CREDITS
Cover© Peter Kunasz; pg 4 © The Final Image; pg 5 © Studio Araminta, Sally Scott; pg 6© Pichugin Dmitry; pg 7 © Koval, Jarno Gonzalez Zarraonandia, NASA; pg 8© Kropotov Andrey, Tatiana Grozetskaya, Juan David Ferrando Subero, Silvio Verrecchia, Victoria Short; pg 9© Thierry Maffeis, Stephanie Dankof; pg 10© Albert Barr, Calin Tatu; pg 11© Yury Zakharov, Dmitry Kosterev; pg 12© Alicia Shields; pg 13© Phdpsx, Roger Pilkington; pg 14© Milan M Jurkovic, Ron Hilton; pg 15© Peter Hansen; pg 16© Steve Cukrov, Greg Henshall, Jocelyn Augustino; pg 17© Graham Prentice; pg 19© Steve Cukrov; pg 20© Ismael Montero Verdu; pg 21-22© Library of Congress; pg 24© dlsphotos; pg 23© Gerald Bernard, Jörg Jahn; pg 26© Sasha Radosavljevich; pg 27 © Donald Joski, Emin Kuliyev, Tim Zurowski

Page 30 Illustration: Erik Courtney

Design and Production - Blue Door Publishing; bdpublishing.com

Library of Congress Cataloging-in-Publication Data

Sepehri, Sandy.
  Rivers / Sandy Sepehri.
    p. cm. -- (Landforms)
  ISBN 978-1-60044-546-0 (Hard cover)
  ISBN 978-1-60044-707-5 (Soft cover)
  1. Rivers--Juvenile literature. I. Title.
  GB1203.8.S47 2008
  551.48'30973--dc22

                                2007012292

Printed in the USA

IG/IG

Table of Contents

What Is a River?   4

The Parts of a River   7

A River's Journey   11

How Rivers Sculpt the Land   12

The Importance of Rivers in America   21

Rivers in Danger   26

Major American Rivers   29

Glossary   31

Index   32

What Is a River?

A river is a large body of water that flows across land and out to another body of water, usually an ocean or sometimes a river or major lake. The rivers of the United States come in a variety of sizes, shapes, and strengths. Some are forceful **rapids**, powerful enough to rip huge boulders from land, while others are gently flowing, peaceful spots for swimming and fishing.

RIVER TRIVIA

Rivers normally flow on the surface of land, but there are also underground rivers that flow within chambers, caves, or caverns.

The Mississippi-Missouri combination is the fourth longest river in the world, at 3,710 miles (5,790 km). The world's longest river is the Nile, in Egypt, on the continent of Africa. The Nile is 4,145 miles (6,670 km) long.

What's **the difference between a river and a lake?**

A river is a flowing body of water, traveling from land, usually out to an ocean. A lake is a body of water surrounded by land, so it doesn't flow out to another body of water.

Farmers use river water to water their crops.

More than 250,000 rivers course their way through the United States, covering about 3,500,000 miles (5,632,704 km)—that's about 140 times around the Earth, at the equator. Rivers are important because they provide the **fresh water** needed for drinking, irrigating (watering) crops, tending farm animals, waste drainage, electrical power, and transportation. Eighty percent of the fresh water used in the United States irrigates crops and generates electric power.

Did You Know? The United States consumes water at twice the rate of other industrialized nations?

How do Rivers Form?

Rivers, and all the water on Earth, begin with **precipitation**, meaning rain and snow. Precipitation is part of the water cycle, also called the hydrologic cycle. Some precipitation seeps underground into the groundwater supply, but most flows across the land into crevasses and cracks to become **creeks**. Eventually, creeks join together into streams; and when streams flow together, they become rivers.

1. Rain and snow fall from clouds to the Earth as precipitation.
2. The sun's heat turns the water into water vapor, through a process called **evaporation**.
3. The water vapor rises and collects into clouds. The water vapor condenses into droplets, and returns to the earth as rain or snow.

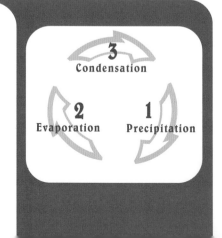

The Parts of a River

Like a board game, a river has a starting place and an ending place. The place where it starts is called its **source**. A river's source is usually a spring, snowfall or rainfall, high up in the hills.

Rain falls in the mountains.

Water from rain, springs, creeks, and glacial meltwater runs across land and eventually drains into creeks, streams, rivers, and lakes. The land over which this water runs is called a river basin, or watershed. The river basin or watershed often feeds the water into the ocean where the river ends.

Underground spring water rises to start a river.

The **Mississippi-Missouri river basin** is the third largest in the world, covering about 40% of the United States and about one-eighth of North America.

Can you name this famous river basin in the Western United States?

Washington

Pacific Ocean

Astoria

Oregon

Spring water bubbles into cracks and forms small creeks, also called the river's headwaters. These creeks meet downhill and form streams and tributaries. Eventually, the streams and tributaries flow together as one river. Together, rivers and streams weave a web of water flowing from mountains to oceans. This web is called a river system.

SPRINGS AND RAIN FEED SMALL CREEKS

CREEKS FEED INTO LARGER TRIBUTARIES AND RIVERS

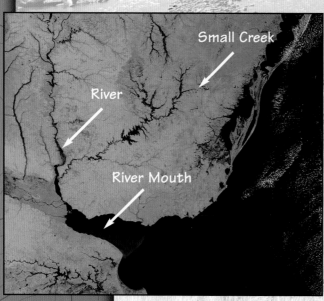

Small Creek

River

River Mouth

This satellite image shows the beginning and end of a river.

SMALL RIVERS FLOW INTO LARGER RIVERS AND THE LARGER RIVERS FLOW INTO OCEANS

The flow of a river is its current. The path a river's current follows is called its course. As it follows its course, a river picks up rocks, stones, and gravel, called its load. After many years, a river's load scrapes and **erodes** the underlying ground, called the riverbed.

The river's course usually ends at the **river's mouth** where the river meets the ocean. The part of the mouth that opens into the ocean is called an **estuary**.

A California river creates a sandy estuary before ending at the Pacific Ocean.

A lighthouse stands at Thomas Point in the Chesapeake Bay to warn ships of shallow waters and rocks.

The largest estuary in the United States is the Chesapeake Bay. Surrounded by Virginia and Maryland, more than 150 rivers and streams drain into the bay, including the major American river, the James River. One of the features of the bay are the Calvert Cliffs, the result of receding waters millions of years ago.

The bay is also home to a large population of land animals as well as fresh and salt water fish.

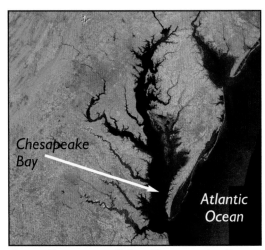

Chesapeake Bay

Atlantic Ocean

A satellite view of the Chesapeake Bay shows the tributaries and rivers that make this bay so large.

In an estuary, fresh river water mixes with salty ocean water—making **brackish water**. Many plants and animals have adapted to life in brackish water, including wood storks, pelicans, and sea lions.

A River's Journey

Like people, rivers are most active when they're young and they slow down when they're old. At the beginning of its existence, usually high on a mountain, a young river rushes downhill, spurred on by gravity and tearing at anything in its way. It is steep, with narrow, deep channels and very few tributaries. It gushes over rocks with such force that it is whipped into foam, called whitewater.

After a river has flowed down from the hills, onto flatter lands, it becomes a slower, mature river. A mature river is fed by many tributaries and its channels erode wider rather than deeper. When it reaches the end of its journey, it becomes an old river. An old river moves slowly into the ocean.

How Rivers Sculpt the Land

The constant flow of a river erodes the land and carries bits of it downstream. Through this process, rivers deliver soil to new areas, making them suitable for plants and animals. Erosion also creates a wide variety of landforms, including **waterfalls**, valleys, canyons, floodplains, **meanders**, **oxbow lakes**, **braids**, and **deltas**. Many of these landforms are famous landmarks in the United States.

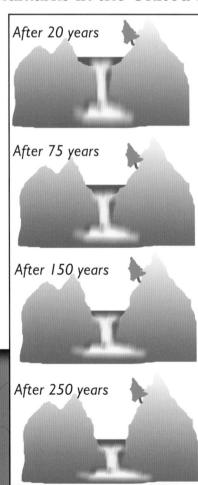

After 20 years

After 75 years

After 150 years

After 250 years

Erosion (i RUH zhuhn)

The process of eroding or being eroded by wind, water, or other natural causes.

River water can erode sand, dirt, and rock. The softer the surface, the quicker it will erode.
This illustration shows the amount of time it would take for water to erode rock and create a gorge.

What kind of water is created when salty ocean water mixes with fresh water?
When these two types of water mix, you get a mix called brackish water.

Waterfalls

A waterfall is the result of a river flowing over the crestline of a cliff. Waterfalls are all different sizes. Some are tall and some are small. Some are very big and powerful.

Niagara Falls, New York.

The most powerful waterfall in North America is Niagara Falls, located on the Niagara River, between the United States and Canada. The crest is 182 feet (55 m) above water level. From it flows about four million cubic feet of water each minute—that's one and a half million gallons (1,892,665 liters) of water per second.

What's a cubic foot of water?
A cubic foot of water is one foot wide, one foot long and one foot high and is equal to 7.48 gallons (28 lit) of water.

ONE FOOT
ONE FOOT
ONE FOOT

Akaka Falls, Hawaii

Valleys

A valley is a low-lying area of land that has been carved by a river. Rivers carve valleys because the surrounding land has a high slope, such as hills and mountains. This slope increases the speed and **turbulence** of the river, which over time, erodes the underlying land into a V-shaped gorge. Valleys range from a few square miles to thousands of square miles in area.

Canyons and Gorges

Sometimes rivers cut through heavy rock and carve out a very deep, steep-walled, V-shaped valley called a canyon. Canyons are usually carved in the upper courses of rivers, where currents are strongest. A gorge is a similar looking, but narrower valley. The largest and most famous canyons are in **arid** or semi-arid lands where there is little rainfall to erode the steep walls.

Farmers take advantage of the rich soil that floodplains create.

Floodplains

The flat land on either side of a river is called its floodplain. When rivers flood, they deposit soil on the floodplains, which can become fertile lands for growing crops. When there is a lot of rain or quickly melted snow, floodplains rise up with water, in other words—flood.

Levees are embankments (walls) built along some areas of rivers to hold back rising floodplain water from dry land.

Levee

Levees have been built all across the United States. Levees are built to protect people and property.

In 2005 hurricane Katrina hit the Gulf Coast. The levees protecting the city of New Orleans broke under the pressure after too much water collected in the canals and rivers. The city flooded, killing and injuring many of the residents.

A river meanders or changes course many times over its life. A river or flowing water will always take the path of less resistance.

Meanders

The curve of a river is called a meander. A meandering river looks like a giant snake from above. Rivers often meander along the middle course of their journey. As a river meanders, it carves away at the shoreline, picking up sediment and dropping it in new locations. This action changes a river's course and its direction.

This satellite photo shows how a river meanders across the land.

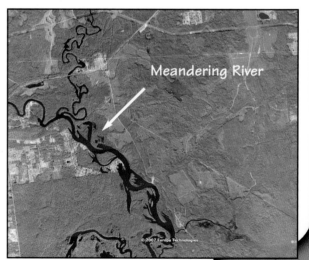

Meandering River

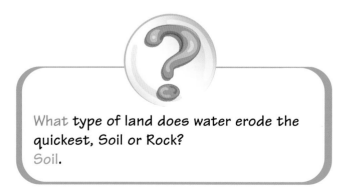

What **type of land does water erode the quickest, Soil or Rock?**
Soil.

Oxbow Lakes

A river meanders around land, creating loops of water. Sometimes a river will cut straight across one of these loops, to shorten its path. When this happens, the curve of water left behind becomes an oxbow lake, also called a bayou in the Mississippi region. If only one curve of water is cut off, it becomes a lake in the shape of the letter C. If more than one curve is cut off, the lake becomes shaped like a serpent.

A beautiful and old oxbow lake near the Teton Mountains in Wyoming.

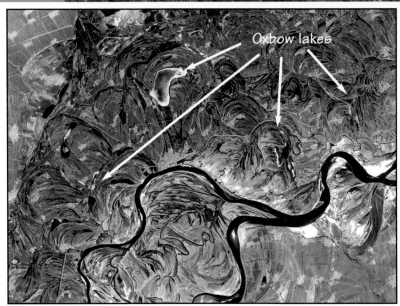

Oxbow lakes

Several oxbow lakes created by a meandering river can be seen in this satellite photograph.

Braids

A shallow river, dotted with many small islands of sand or pebbles, has to split into different channels to go around these islands. When this happens, the various river channels appear braided, like long strands of hair made of water. The small islands causing the braided effect are called braid bars and are often temporary since the river continually picks up and moves sand and sediment.

Deltas

When a river finally reaches the end of its journey, at its mouth, it is no longer a whitewater gush, rushing down a mountain. Now it is an old river, slowly moving towards the ocean. At the place where it meets the ocean, there is usually a large area of very fine sand, called silt, over which it must split into many different channels. This area of muddy land is called a delta.

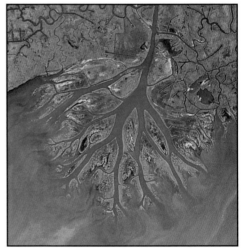

As it nears the ocean, the Mississippi River creates a giant delta made up of large siltbed islands and river channels.

The Importance of Rivers in America

The first towns and farms of pioneer settlers were established along riverfronts and floodplains. Rivers and streams provided the settlers with drinking water, transportation, and power to run their mills and factories. The floodplains were fertile lands for their crops because, when rivers flood, they bring nutrient-rich soil to their floodplains.

Rivers were both important and dangerous to settlers. While searching for places to settle down, families and their livestock had to get across rivers, often with deep and swift currents. Oxen pulled wagons across shallow rivers. For fast-moving rivers, settlers placed their wagon, animals, and family upon a large, flat boat called a scow. Sometimes, Native Americans would ferry settlers across for payment or trade.

People on a ferry crossing the Red River, Texas 1874.

Scow - flat boat

RIVER TRIVIA

Crossing a river in the 1800s could take as long as five days.

Rivers are still very important in America because they are a primary source of fresh water that we use for drinking, farming, and spinning turbines to generate electricity. The quality of a community's river has a big impact on the quality of its jobs, economy, recreation, and culture. To help restore and protect American rivers, the United States has created a program called The American Heritage Rivers Initiative, which provides federal assistance to help communities clean up and protect their rivers.

Can you name a large river near where you live?

Throughout the United States, 14 rivers have been selected as American Heritage Rivers. For each of these rivers, the federal government selected a contact person called a 'river navigator.' This person helps his or her community receive federal and private resources (money) for cleaning their river water and creating employment opportunities associated with their river.

1. Blackstone and Woonasquatucket Rivers (Massachusetts, Rhode Island)
2. Connecticut River (Connecticut, Vermont, New Hampshire, Massachusetts)
3. Cuyahoga River (Ohio)
4. Detroit River (Massachusetts)
5. Hanalei River (Hawaii)
6. Hudson River (New York)
7. Lower Mississippi River (Louisiana, Tennessee)

8. New River (North Carolina, Virginia, West Virginia)
9. Potomac River (District of Columbia, Maryland, Pennsylvania, Virginia, West Virginia)
10. Rio Grande River (Texas)
11. St. Johns River (Florida)
12. Upper Mississippi River (Iowa, Illinois, Minnesota, Missouri)
13. Upper Susquehanna and Lackawanna Rivers (Pennsylvania)
14. Willamette River (Oregon)

People have not taken care of rivers over the past years. Everyone should take care not to litter.

Rivers in Danger

When rivers flow downstream, they not only pick up silt and minerals from the soil and rock in the riverbed, they also pick up pollutants, including animal waste, human sewage, pesticides, and chemical runoff from farms, factories, and urban areas. The resulting polluted rivers are unsafe for swimming and fishing and for animal habitats. People are also affected by eating contaminated fish caught in polluted rivers.

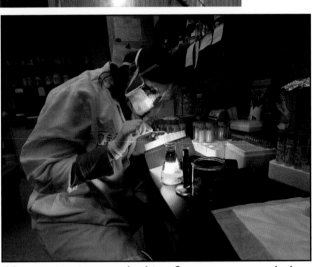

Many scientists are looking for new ways to help protect our rivers, lakes, and oceans.

RIVER TRIVIA

Did You Know? One half of the 1,200 threatened or endangered animal species depend upon rivers and streams.

Major Rivers — Major Rivers

○ — River Label

Major American Rivers

Below is a list of 24 major rivers in the United States:

1. Arkansas, 1,460 miles (2,349 km) (flows into Mississippi River)
2. Brazos, 1,280 miles (2,059 km) (flows into Gulf of Mexico)
3. Canadian, 906 miles (1,458 km) (flows into Arkansas River)
4. Chattahoochee
5. Colorado, 1,450 miles (2,350 km) (flows into Gulf of California)
6. Connecticut
7. Columbia, 1,240 miles (1,995 km) (flows into Pacific Ocean)
8. Gila, 630 miles (1,013 km) (flows into Colorado River)
9. Green, 730 miles (1,174 km) (flows into Colorado River)
10. Illinoise
11. Mississippi, 2,340 miles (3,765 km) (flows into Gulf of Mexico)
12. Missouri, 2,540 miles (4,087 km) (flows into Mississippi River)
13. Ohio, 981 miles (1,578 km) (flows into Mississippi River)
14. Pecos, 926 miles (1,490 km) (flows into Gulf of Mexico)
15. Platte, 990 miles (1,593 km) (flows into Missouri River)
16. Red, 1,290 miles (2,076 km) (flows into Mississippi River)
17. Rio Grande, 1,900 miles (3,057 km) (flows into Gulf of Mexico)
18. Sacramento
19. San Joaquin
20. Snake, 1,040 miles (1,673 km) (flows into Missouri River)
21. Susquehanna
22. Tennessee, 866 miles (1,393 km) (flows into Ohio River)
23. Wabash
24. Yellowstone, 692 miles (1,113 km) (flows into Missouri River)

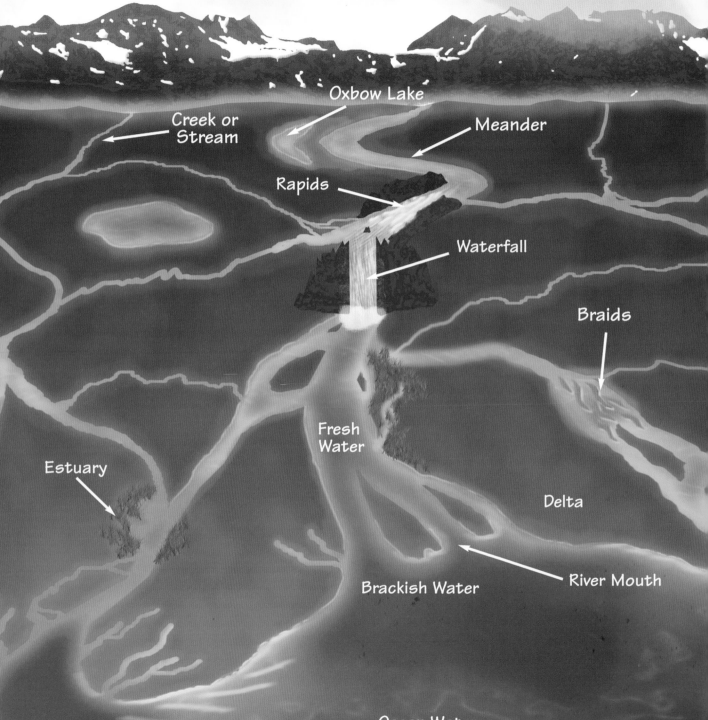

Rain Fall

Oxbow Lake

Creek or
Stream

Meander

Rapids

Waterfall

Braids

Fresh
Water

Estuary

Delta

Brackish Water

River Mouth

Ocean Water

Glossary

arid (a rid) — dry; having little or no rainfall

brackish water (BRAK ish - WAW tur) — fresh river water mixed with salty ocean water

braids (BRAYDZ) — small river channels created by sand or pebbles

creek (KREEK) — a natural stream of water smaller than a river and often a tributary of a river

delta (DEL tuh) — an area of muddy land where a river meets the ocean

erode (i RODE) — to wear or wash away

estuary (ESS choo er ee) — the part of the river mouth that opens into the ocean

evaporation (i VAP uh ray chun) — the process by which a liquid changes into a gas

fresh water (FRESH WAW tur) — water that is not salty

meander (mee AN dur) — the curve of a river

oxbow lake (OKS bo lak) — a lake created by a river cutting through a meander

precipitation (pri SIP i tay shuhn) — water falling from the sky as rain, sleet, or snow

rapids (RAP idz) — a fast-moving part of a river created by a steep slope in the riverbed

river mouth (RIV ur - mouth) — the end of a river's course

source (SORSS) — where a river begins, usually on high ground where runoff collects or a spring surfaces

turbulence (TUR byuh lens) — irregular, or swirling movement of water

waterfall (WAW tur fawl) — a place where a river falls from a height

Index

American Heritage Rivers   23, 24
brackish water   10, 12, 30
braids   12, 19, 30
channels   11, 19, 20
current   9, 15, 22
delta   12, 20, 30
estuary   9, 10, 30
floodplains 12, 16, 21
gorges   15
groundwater   6
headwaters   8

load   9
meander   12, 17, 18, 30
mouth   8, 9, 20, 30
oxbow lakes   12, 18, 30
river system   8
riverbed   9, 26
tributary   8
valleys   12, 14
water cycle   6
waterfalls   12, 13
watershed   7

Further Reading

Green, Emily. *Rivers*. Children's Press, 2006.
Morris, Neil. *Living by Rivers*. The Creative Company, 2004.
Ross, Mandy. *Rivers*. The Creative Company, 2004.

Websites To Visit

www.americanrivers.org
www.nationalgeographic.com/geographyaction/rivers/
www.riverkeeper.org

About the Author

Sandy Sepehri lives with her husband, Shahram, and their three children
in Florida. She has a bachelor's degree and writes freelance articles and
children's stories. She has also written a number of fiction and
nonfiction books.